# THE ART OF THE ONE CALL CLOSE

# THE ART OF THE ONE CALL CLOSE

A Sale of Five or Five Million...

Learn How to Walk in And Walk Out with The Real Deal!

Freddy Freundlich

Copyright © 2020 Freddy Freundlich

All rights reserved. This book or any portion thereof may not be reproduced or used in any manner whatsoever without the express written permission of the publisher except for the use of brief quotations in a book review.

Printed by Kindle Direct Publishing in the United States of America
First printing, 2020

ISBN: 978-1-7338955-1-4

www.rabbifreddy.com

This book is dedicated to Lesley, no need to say more...

# Table of Contents

Foreword ............................................................................................. 1

Chapter 1 – I Love action and I love money ................................. 3

Chapter 2 – Sales is about relationships ....................................... 7

Chapter 3 – What's a one-call close? ........................................... 14

Chapter 4 – What qualifies as a one-call close? ......................... 17

Chapter 5 – Can anything be closed in one call? ....................... 20

Chapter 6 – Why is it so important to become a ...................... 23

Chapter 7 – Selling is a science, it's not magic .......................... 29

Chapter 8 – Let's get down to business! ..................................... 33

Chapter 9 – WIIFM ......................................................................... 36

Chapter 10 – Assumptive close .................................................... 39

Chapter 12 – Open .......................................................................... 44

Chapter 13 – Middle ....................................................................... 50

Chapter 14 – Close .......................................................................... 56

Chapter 15 – Objections ................................................................. 63

Chapter 16 – Money Objections ................................................... 70

Chapter 18 – It's all about today! ................................................. 78

# THE ART OF THE ONE CALL CLOSE

x

# Foreword

At the end of the day, one thing is certain... People only want what's good for them. They want to feel good, to feel that they got exactly what they want, that they got the best deal, and that they made the right decision. They want to feel that they've bought, not that they were sold. They want to feel really good, to be really proud of their purchase, and they want this feeling to continue tomorrow, the following day, throughout the week, and the week after... People want everyone around them, whether it's their boss, coworker, spouse, partner, friend, or anyone really, to believe that they got a great deal.

Your utmost concern should be making sure that your prospect feels good. And you need to understand that all he/she really cares about is, "what's in it for me?" It's never about you, or your problems, your dreams, your kids, least of all, your marital problems. It's all about them, you are irrelevant. So, your number one priority, at all times, should be to make that prospect in front of you feel good, and if you want a better result, make them feel great! The better you are at doing this, the more successful you will be. Could anything be simpler than this? Why would anyone want to make it tough? Now, if this is all true, then your business is not selling, rather it is making people feel good. The question to ask yourself is, am I capable of doing this very simple thing? Of course, there's a little more to it, but not much. The rest is technical. Simply, is he or she a qualified buyer?

If you are ready to accept this thesis, then the first and most important thing for you to do is, to sell yourself on yourself. Do you feel good? Are you in a good place? How do you define yourself! If I was right in front of you, and you had just sixty seconds to impress me, will you be able to provide a sixty-second elevator pitch about who you are? Or what you can do for me? Because if you only have sixty seconds to impress me, what would you think is more important to me? Hearing about you, or about how you can improve my life? Seems pretty obvious, but sadly, it's not. This is simply what separates the great salesperson from the mediocre salesperson, in other words, the 80/20 rule.

As soon as I started to write this book, I knew right away that I had a challenge on my hands. I wanted to share how simple one-call closing is, could be, and should be. Indeed, closing a sale in one call sounds like it should be sweet and short, and that's what I knew this book had to be. My challenge was that traditional book publishers want a book to be at least fifty thousand words, and I knew I'd be lucky to get to half of that. I could always add lots of fluff, but that would defeat the purpose. A book on one-call closing in sales, should be simple and easy to read.

So here it is, a book you can get through in one sitting, because what I've got to share with you is just that; simple and easy. This is not complicated; it's not rocket science or brain surgery. It's just about learning how to have better conversations and developing a certain mindset. In order to be a one-call closer, you only need two abilities. First, you should know how to have a conversation? Secondly, knowing how to be specific about what you want.

This book has only one goal, and that's for you to make more money! For this to happen, you will need to close more sales; faster, easier, and with less cost and aggravation. To sum it up, if within thirty days of reading this book, you're not closing more sales than you are now, then, one of us has really screwed up. But then again, what's the chance of that happening?

# Chapter 1 –
# I love action and I love money

I love action and I love money, and that's why I got into sales. That being said, I have no patience, and no appreciation for delayed gratification. I want my cake and I want to eat it too. Right now!
I was blessed because my first real sales job was not for an IBM, Xerox, or some other heavy hitter, it was for a sign company. I went door-to-door all over the United States selling outdoor neon lighted signs, to small and medium-sized businesses.

The reason I say I was blessed, because it was one of the hardest sales jobs one could ever do. Not only was it a cold call, door-to-door sell, but we were expected to close the deal in just one sales call. We didn't even carry business cards. There was no reason. If we didn't close the sale on that first visit, we were never going back. This job was only for the brave and the bold, as it was one hundred percent commission-based. No salary, no draw, and as for expenses, I had to cover them all out of my own pocket. Most of the people who started this job didn't last out a week, but those of us who did, made some really great money. It was the early eighties; I was young and single with no responsibilities. Nobody to tell me what I ought to be doing, so I traveled all over the country having loads of fun and making a ton of money.

When I was first offered this job, I was very apprehensive. As a college graduate, I expected a job with a big salary, maybe selling pharmaceuticals, or perhaps advertising. I'd been selling stuff since I was ten years old, so I knew what it meant to be a salesman. As a kid selling small stuff like newspapers and candy, a one-call close was almost a given. However, for something that cost hundreds, or even thousands of dollars, I couldn't have believed it possible to close in one meeting. Everybody I knew offered their two cents telling me I was crazy to even consider a commissioned-sales job, let alone one in which the sale was expected to be closed in one call.

Maybe I was, crazy, but I was also ambitious. "Dumb and hungry" with everyone who "knew what was good for me," telling me I was nuts to even consider taking this type of job, I drank the Kool-Aid. Of course, I was enticed by the opportunity to travel and make money. Lots and lots of money! I figured if others could do it, why couldn't I? So, since I hadn't yet been jaded with what was, or wasn't possible, I took the job and ran with it.

Living in Denver, Colorado, every Sunday evening, a bunch of us would hit the road and drive to any town in the USA, and check into the nicest motel we could find. The next morning, we'd all meet for breakfast, pump each other up, go over a map of the area, and then, head out to our assigned areas. Door-to-door, store-to-store, I'd ask to speak with the owner. After introducing myself, I'd find out if they had any partners. If all the decision-makers were present, I'd then make my presentation. Depending on how well things turned out, about a couple of hours later, I'd often find myself walking out with a signed agreement and a twenty-five percent cash deposit.

Sale or not, no matter what happened, I never returned. They trained us to do whatever it took, but we weren't to leave without a decision, either a yes or no!

I know this might sound crazy for a lot of people. You might even be thinking; sounds good, but it won't work in my industry. Or even if it might work, certainly not for a high-ticket item, maybe for something less expensive. Well, I've been there, I thought the same thing. I had no doubt I could walk in and out with a closed sale, if we were talking about maybe a few hundred dollars, but a few thousand? Well, to my very pleasant surprise, I was closing deals for as much as five thousand dollars, and this was 1980s dollars, which today is worth almost fifteen thousand dollars. Okay, but maybe you sell stuff in the six-figure region, or maybe, even as high as seven-figures. Nobody would ever make a final decision, in just a couple of hours, for that kind of money, but in fact they did. To be sure, even though I was doing it, I wasn't totally convinced either. I figured it would only work sometimes, or up to a certain amount of money.

That being said, life was good for me, in fact, really fantastic. I loved the sales profession, and this job was fantastic. I had freedom, flexibility, and unlimited earning power.

Being ambitious, I wanted to make even more money, and started to look for a better job. Having gained so much experience in the art of one-call closing, I was drawn to similar jobs. The one difference was that as I moved from one position to another, it was always for a larger ticket item than the one before, which made me more money.

One day, I was offered a position with an advertising company who claimed that their services could be closed in one call. I always heard this because everyone wanted a real one-call closer, but the truth was that most companies weren't always what they claimed to be. One of the beautiful things about being a professional one-call closer is that you are in the driver's seat. You get to decide which job you want to take, and not the other way around. This particular company claimed that their average sale was in the neighborhood of forty thousand dollars, sometimes as much as one hundred thousand dollars. I was sure they were pulling my leg. First off, besides the cost, this was for a service, not even a product. Secondly, the buyers were some of the most notoriously known conservative people in the business world, the last type of people who would ever make an impulsive decision – bankers. As it turned out, I was wrong.

For three years, I sold advertising packages to small and medium-sized banks and credit unions all across North America. Almost all of them were one-call closes. The one caveat, I will add, is that while they were mostly one-call closes, they weren't cold calls. I would have telemeters cold-call them and set up appointments for me. But once I was in the door, not only would I end up walking out with a contract, but with a hefty check in hand.

# Chapter 2 –
# Sales is about relationships

Sales is about helping people and companies! It's not about forcing people to buy things they don't want nor need. I take pride in the fact that I help people and companies make decisions on products or services that make their lives, and businesses, more efficient.

Closing a sale in one call is not about tricking the client or pressuring them to buy something they don't need. In fact, it's the opposite! When the sales cycle drags on, it wastes everybody's time. A professional one-call closer is not necessarily about making the sale in one meeting, it's about getting a real decision made in that meeting. A professional one-call closer doesn't care if he or she gets a "no", as long as it's a real "no".

**So, what's our goal?**

Our only goal is for you to make more money. That being said, before we can discuss making more money, we need to know what our commodity is? Oh, I can hear you saying, that's really simple, I sell XYZ. Yes, that's what you're selling, but it's not your commodity. We all sell different things, yet we have one commodity in common, and that's time!

When we talk about having more time in our lives. We're not just talking about our business life, but also our personal lives. I am repeating myself, but this is the first cardinal rule you must internalize. Time is a commodity! It's the only commodity we all share equally. No matter who you are or where you're from, it makes no difference, you have the same amount of time as anyone else. Yes, believe it or not, there is something that you and the wealthiest person on this planet have in common. Twenty-four-hours-a-day. And you both have to use from within these hours for your personal needs. This means a reduction in the number of usable working hours. The one major difference between both of you is the value of those hours. His or her hours are worth more than yours. Remember time is a commodity, limited and variable. Whether your time is worth one million dollars per hour, or two dollars an hour, you can't change the number of hours at your disposal, but you can change the value of those hours. The more you can accomplish in your "available" hours, the more the worth of your hour. Of course, not everything is about money, there is also quality of life, but regardless, your hours are limited. So, how many of your hours do you want to spend on generating revenue? And how many hours do you want to spend on quality of life? Ideally, you'd like them to be one and the same. Regardless of your answer, remember you've still only got twenty-four-hours-a-day, and that's all inclusive.

We now know a number of things. First, your time is limited. You have only so many hours in a day and that fact will never change. Secondly, you want your limited hours to produce as much revenue as possible. Lastly, you want to be happy and enjoy your life. That's it! That's what you and I want.

According to the latest United Nations census, there are about 7.7 billion people on planet Earth. That's a lot of people, and a lot of prospects, no matter what you're selling. It doesn't matter what your product or service is; you have somebody out there who wants what you are selling. Regardless of your potential prospects, the one absolute fact is that you only have one hundred and sixty-eight hours in your week. Even if you work sixty-hours-a-week, you have a finite number of hours. Why is it that there are people who only work twenty hours per week, who earn tons more than people who work sixty hours per week? Are they smarter? Not necessarily, but they probably work smarter. So, even though knowing how to sell and close a deal is important, knowing how to manage your time, and quantify your hours are equally as important. It doesn't matter if you can close nine out of ten people, if you're not able to maximize your hourly earning potential, you are sabotaging yourself.

**You need to focus on the prospects with most potential**

You must spend time qualifying your prospect. So many salespeople convince themselves that they are really working by just going through the numbers, but that's not how it works in real life. Being busy doesn't make you money, being busy with the right prospect does.

Remember that sales are easy if you have the right prospect. If you don't invest your time in qualifying your prospects, you will end up banging your head against the wall. You'll get frustrated quickly and burn out. You will then insist you are a terrible salesperson, but the truth is that you never gave yourself a chance.

With 7.7 billion people out there, why waste time on low potential prospects? Speak to any successful salesperson, and they will tell you it is almost always easier to get the bigger deal, than the smaller one. Always focus on the prospect who has the most potential to buy whatever it is you are selling. Even if they end up spending less than you originally envisioned, you have a much better chance that they will buy. You always have a better chance of making the sale, with a top gun than the opposite.

Now, what about the proverbial salesperson who is so good, that he can sell ice to an Eskimo. The truth is no good salesperson would waste their valuable time trying to sell ice to an Eskimo. With 7.7 billion prospects, wouldn't it make more sense to sell ice to a person who lives in the Sahara Desert? Make sure the prospect needs your product!

Regardless of what you're selling, all 7.7 billion people are not prospects for you, but then again, I'm sure, by now, you're getting the point. You've got a large volume of prospects. You should also be conscious of the fact that whatever the number of prospects you have out of this 7.7 billion, some of them may be just a part of the decision process, while others will be sole decision-makers. If only one person is a qualified buyer, then your job is easier.

But then again, is this really true? Not necessarily. Humans are indecisive creatures. Many times, people don't trust themselves, and will feel more comfortable getting reinforcement from a trusted friend or peer. Also, when there is more than one prospect, they create a dynamic, a momentum, a certain amount of synergy which makes the sale go smoother. In fact, buyer's remorse is considerably lower when a sale has been made to more than one person. Either way, there are pros and cons to having a single prospect or multiple. The most important thing is that when you make your presentation, you have all the decision-makers in front of you, and that they are all qualified.

Different products and services, different people and companies. Whether you present to a group, couple, or individual, the question should be, "where will I invest my time?" The answer is simple... "Where am I going to get the biggest bang for my buck!"

There are many different variables, but always use the cardinal rule. What will give you the biggest bang for your buck?

10

In order to do this, you must have stock. Stock? I don't have a retail store; I don't even have products; I sell a service. Stock for a salesperson are prospects, and the storage for your stock is a prospecting funnel. A prospecting funnel is not the same as a sales funnel. A sales funnel starts with a qualified buyer, while a prospecting funnel starts with anybody. You may already have a job or a business in which your prospects are already qualified buyers, which is fine. But if you don't, and you truly want to be a successful salesperson, you will need a good prospecting tool.

Always invest in the best tools for your business. Never be cheap on your trading tools, be it clothes, equipment, a computer program, or anything else your business requires.

Let me take this moment to give you some very valuable advice. If you don't already have a good CRM (customer relationship management) program, get one right away. I don't care what your product or service is, if you don't have a great CRM program, it's similar to running a marathon with only one leg. You are handicapping yourself unnecessarily.
When I first got into sales, years ago, one of my mentors told me… Beg, borrow, or steal, buy the best suit and car you can. Today, many sales are done virtually so this same sage advice may not apply, but I am sure if my mentor were alive today, he would have added a great CRM. It is the most important tool you will need to help you manage your time and pipeline.

For a salesperson who starts from scratch, not having a prospecting funnel is the equivalent of a mechanic without a toolbox. No matter how good they are, there's bound to be a limit to how efficient they will be at getting the job done. A good CRM will take the raw material, which at this point are suspects, put them in the funnel, take them through the various stages, and at the end, turn them into qualified prospects.

A qualified prospect is made up of two primary ingredients. First, have they already shown prior interest in what you're selling? Or will you be able to provide them with a reason to want your product or service, even if at first, they don't see it?

Then, second, is he/she the decision-maker, and do they have the qualifications you are looking for? Let's be honest. Without a doubt, there may be some people who earn minimum wages, yet drive luxury cars, but then again, why would you want to invest your valuable time specifically going after these people?

Now, even if you are a salesperson with qualified leads from a prospecting funnel, don't think your job is easier and it's all match and go. This is not always the case. It strongly depends on how good your prospect feeder is. Regardless of how you get your qualified leads, I would suggest you re-qualify them yourself. There is nothing worse for a professional salesperson than to invest so much time and energy into a sales presentation, only to find out that you just blew your wad for nothing. So, instead of flying in blindly, it's much wiser to invest a little extra time to re-qualify a prospect, than to rely on someone or something out of your control. Why don't most salespeople re-qualify? Because it scares them! They're afraid they'll lose the sale. Please remember, if you lose the sale by re-qualifying, then you never had it in the first place.

Regardless of how you operate, you want to have both a prospecting funnel, and a sales funnel in your CRM. They are two different and separate entities, but they are as important to your business as a hammer and nails are to a carpenter.

A well-managed CRM will be very heavy at the top and will start out with theoretically as many as 7.7 billion suspects. It will then, very quickly, start turning the unqualified suspects into qualified prospects. Once you have your qualified prospects, you can, then, move them over to your sales funnel.

Imagine, instead of people, we were talking about grains of sand or bits of coal? Or we can even go further back and start with pre-coal; dirt and water which have coalesced over years. Your qualified prospect is similar to a beautiful polished diamond. But that diamond started out as nothing more than dirt and water. It took a lot of time, but over many moons this dirt made the transition to coal, etc. until it finally became a diamond. Even than it was not the same polished diamond which ended up on your finger. Just like this diamond had to go through a lot of different stages, so will your unqualified suspects, as they slowly turn into qualified prospects. Of course, the big difference is that it won't take millions of years.

# Chapter 3 –
# What's a one-call close?

Before we go any further, let's qualify ourselves.

The first and most important thing that it takes to be a one-call closer is the belief that it's even possible. Let's first ignore the possibility of whether or not you believe, you can personally close a sale on the first call. My question to you is, do you believe that a one-call close is even possible? Again, not necessarily you, but do you think someone could possibly close sales on a regular basis in only one call?

Most people don't believe it's possible, and that's why they never close their deals in the first call. Let's not forget, we already established that very few salespeople are true professionals, let alone one-call closers. Most people who call themselves salespeople are, in the real sense, clerks or order-takers. So, what are you? Do you consider yourself a professional salesperson? Are you proud of what you do? Are you proud of the product or service you sell?

If the answer to any of these questions is no, then perhaps, you should reconsider your profession. Sales is not for everybody and just like most professions, to be truly great, you have to love what you're doing...

I'm glad you're still here! Bravo!

I already defined what a one-call close is, but it's worth repeating because it needs to really sink in. It is making a sale, in other words, closing the deal, in one visit. It doesn't matter whether it's a face-to-face meeting, or a virtual means of communication. The simplest definition of what qualifies as a one-call close is to walk in, make your sales presentation, and walk out with a signed deal. Please, note that a one-call close does not always necessarily mean it literally takes just one meeting. It may very well depend on the size of the deal, industry type, etc.

Does it matter if the product or service that I am selling is a "one-off" sale or a "relationship" sale? What's the difference in the two? The difference should be obvious, but this is a good stepping stone for my next lesson. Never assume anything! What might seem obvious to you, may not be so obvious to the other person. This goes for every relationship that you have. In fact, an acronym for assume is, when you ASS/U/ME, you make an ass out of you and me. This being said, a "one-off" sale involves selling an item or service as a one-time deal. For instance, selling expensive vacuum cleaners door-to-door. Whereas, a relationship sale is more like selling office supplies. This is something that is sold on a recurring basis. You don't want to sell to him just for today, but rather for years to come. I need to reiterate, that life is not black and white, there are always exceptions to every rule. For instance, if you sell cars, is that a one-off or a relationship type of sale? In truth, it could be a bit of both.

It doesn't matter which type of sale this is, your initial goal is the same, to walk in, present, and leave with a done deal in hand. It is just as important to close that relationship client on the first call as it is to close the one-off client. The difference is that your long-term goals are different. With a one-off, you want to sell as much as you can, upsell, and upgrade whatever you can, because once the ball game is over, it's over. For instance, if you're selling automobiles, you don't want to say, okay, I'll just sell him the basic model and on my next visit, I'll upsell him to a more deluxe model.

You will not say to him, don't worry about air conditioning, I will catch you next time. No, it's neither to your benefit nor the customer's. You need to outfit him with the best you can, right now.

When your primary purpose is to "get your foot in the door," then, your aim, today, is to sell anything, no matter how small. If you are selling cleaning supplies and the business has 50,000 employees, I understand you have dreams of grandeur and want all of their business. If you're like me, you want it now, today! Chances are, though, you won't get it! Instead, go for the immediate sale today, anything you can get! Unless they are just opening their doors, it means they are already dealing with at least one supplier and I am sure they haven't run out of toilet paper. You're also probably one of the dozens of salespeople who want their business and claim that their toilet paper is nicer, smoother, and cheaper than everybody else's. Forget about all this today, just make a sale and get yourself on their vendor list!

Your aim today is to differentiate yourself from all the others. Your job today is not to make money, it's to become a vendor. It doesn't matter what you sell him today, just sell. One four-pack roll of toilet paper is great. If you can sell a gross, then, go for it, but remember your main aim is to go from just being another of the Wanna-Be's to being a real bona fide vendor.

# Chapter 4 –
# What qualifies as a one-call close?

To make a one-call close sale, you need to have completed your sales presentation. If you completed your sales presentation and didn't walk out with a sale, regardless of what happens next, you didn't make your sale in one call. Sometimes, you may need a preparatory visit, to either gather information, or to arrange for all the decision-makers to be present. And if you are cold calling, you may need a meeting, just to schedule the sales presentation. As long as you haven't completed the sales presentation, you will not have lost the chance to turn the sale into a one-call close.

Here is a good rule of thumb to use... if you've discussed price and walked away without a done deal, then you blew it. What does it mean to close a sale? It means a signature and/or a check. Every industry has its own definition of what makes up closing a deal. You know yours. Closing a deal is final, it's not almost or 99%, it's 100%!

I hope it is now clear to what a one-call close is, or is it? Just to be clear, a one-call close is making one, and only one sales presentation, and then, walking out with a closed deal. This can be a virtual sale or a frontal sale, but you "need to have the check in hand", or its equivalent. There are no if's. It's either you have a sale, or you don't! There is no almost, there are no "come back tomorrow for a second signature," there are no "yes, for sure I want it, but because of my religion, I'll need to pray on it through the night." I don't know how to make this any simpler, a closed deal is a deal in hand!

Right now, you are probably thinking, "I like what I'm reading, but in my business, it's simply not possible." Perhaps you're correct, but I'm willing to place a bet that you could be wrong. Even if you're in one of those few industries where it is indeed almost impossible to close a sale in one meeting, by following my directions, you'll still be able to cut your sales cycle by at least 50%.

I need to be very upfront with you. Most people have very little chance of selling to a prospect in one meeting. Are you shocked? You should be, but that's because most people think they are dealing with a prospect, but in reality, they are really dealing with "suspects."

What's the difference between a prospect and a suspect? A prospect has been qualified and confirmed. Until you have confirmed him or her, they should be seen as a suspect. A prospect is of legal age and can sign the check. Your prospect may also be part of a decision-making team, but alone they are still a suspect. You need to know who else is part of the decision-making process? Is there a spouse, a partner, or a board? Part of your job is to do your homework, and make sure that before you present, you have the qualified buyer, or buyers, present. If all the decision-makers aren't in attendance, your chances of closing the deal, today, or, in fact, ever, is slim to none. No matter how much he or she loves you and your product, you will not sell the "manager," only the boss. The definition of the boss is one who signs the checks!

Simple as this really is, I'm hearing all the "what ifs?". When we talk about decision-makers, there are no "what ifs." If you're not prepared to only present to qualified buyers, then, spare yourself the time wastage and pass this book onto someone else.

Besides having the ability to decide, you need one other thing for a qualified buyer; that is a "need." I personally do not own a television (I believe it's a time-waster). That being said, one day, a salesperson for a local cable company came to my house trying to sell me a subscription to their satellite services. I said, no thank you, I don't own a television. If he had read my book, he'd have said, "thank you for your time," asked me for a referral, and moved on. Instead, this bozo spent thirty minutes trying to convince me on why I was making a mistake and should start watching television. Forget about my time, but he wasted thirty minutes of his own precious time. Time he'll never get back, trying to convince me to change my mind on a principled belief. Yes, there was a very slight chance he might have succeeded, but was it a good investment of his time? This is a rhetorical question; what do you think?

I admit, I'm a rarity. Most people own televisions and use some sort of cable, satellite, or internet provider. How many other doors could he have been knocking on in that half-hour? Sales is not about being right, it's about getting rich. Remember, time is our only fixed commodity, it's all we've got in common. No matter what, we will not sell everybody, it's a numbers game. There are plenty of prospects out there, stop wasting your time on suspects.

# Chapter 5 –
# Can anything be closed in one call?

Theoretically, yes!

The truth though is that, life is not about absolutes. Hence, things have to occur under the right circumstances. What are the right circumstances? Again, very simply, having a qualified buyer and all the decision-makers present. On those occasions when a one-call close is not possible, a one-call closer will still be able to cut the closing process at least in half. If it ordinarily takes you six months to close a deal, a real one-call closer will have that deal signed, sealed, and delivered within three months.

Now that we have accepted the premise that there are certain times and places, where a one-call close might not be quite possible or practical, let's address those sales that can be one-call closed. As with everything in life, there are several caveats. As mentioned earlier, the biggest two are that one can only close a sale in one call if the decision-maker, or makers, are present, and that they are qualified buyers.

One of our biggest challenges, as a one-call closer, is understanding that people do, indeed, make instantaneous decisions. Our job is to help them understand and verbalize that decision whether it's a "yes" or a "no". Once again, a "no" is just as good as a "yes."

Why is a "no" just as good as a "yes?" Well, it's all about your closing number. Let's say your closing number is six, which means you now close six out of ten presentations. This doesn't necessarily mean that out of every ten presentations you will, indeed, close six.

You, in fact, may have to make twenty presentations, and then close twelve. Or perhaps, thirty presentations and close eighteen, but at the end of the day, the numbers will still work out.

One of the most important attributes of being a professional is to be able to accurately define the terms to use. We've been talking about sales calls, but what makes up a sales call? A sales call is when you have made a sales presentation. If you haven't made a full-blown sales presentation, then it doesn't count as a sales call, and as such, can't be factored into your closing number. Only after completing your sales presentation, can the sales call be considered valid for your closing number. Then we want to know, did you receive a genuine "yes" or "no"? "Maybe's" don't count! What this implies is that if half of your presentations end up with some variation of "I need to think about it," or other excuses for not giving you an on-the-spot decision, your closing numbers will take a big hit. Now, you will have to make twenty calls, just to close six. So, in the real sense, your closing number is now only three.
This, my friends, may be one of the hardest concepts for you to understand. I know it's hard, but you're wasting your valuable, precious time if you leave that meeting with anything, but a "yes" or a "no". Now, you should understand that you won't close every deal, and that it doesn't matter, you need to celebrate your "no's" as much as your "yes's". Crazy, huh! Every "no" brings you so much closer to the next "yes," but "maybe's" bring you nothing.

**Remember, real "no's" are worth the same as real "yes's". "Maybe's", "tomorrow," and "I'll think about it," are worth absolutely nothing.**

Let's translate this into facts and figures. Assuming your current closing number is now six, and your average sale commission is one hundred dollars, it means that out of every ten sales calls, you will on average earn six hundred dollars. If we, then, take those six hundred dollars and divide by ten, we now have sixty dollars per call, whether it's a "yes" or a "no".

Take a moment and let this sink in. When you make a sales presentation, whether it's frontal or virtual, you have only three possible results; "yes," "no," or "maybe". A real "yes" or "no" is worth money to you. In fact, using our example, it's worth sixty dollars per presentation, while a "maybe," no matter what the reason, is worth absolutely nothing, zero! No matter how much you want to believe that it will eventually be a "yes," it won't change the numbers.

# Chapter 6 –
# Why is it so important to become a one-call closer?

What if we don't close the sale on the first call? Well, to begin with, the chances of closing the deal, at all, drops in drastic proportions. We just discussed a salesperson's closing number. Remember, the best salesperson in the world won't close every deal, and the worst salesperson in the world will sell something, if he or she makes enough presentations. While a terrible salesperson may only close one deal in a hundred, and a top ace may close nine out of ten, It's all about the numbers.

Here, we are using extreme examples... going from a 1% closing ratio on the one hand, to a 90% closing ratio on the other. Most of us are somewhere in between. Your job, regardless of what your number is, needs to be to improve that number. You only get one number for each prospect, so the more times you return to close the deal, the worse your situation gets. You'll also end up earning less as a result. For example, if you are selling widgets, where the average sales call is one hour, and let's say the average commission earned is $100 per deal. If you close the deal in one visit, then you have made $100 per hour. If it takes you a follow-up visit to close the deal, then you have only made $50 per hour, four visits will be $25, and so forth.

Your prospect will never be hotter than on the first call. Never more ready to buy, than on that first visit. So, not only does your hourly rate decline with each follow-up sales visit, but your money-making potential, in general, declines exponentially.

Take out a blank piece of paper and write across in big letters – 100%. This represents both what you might earn on that first visit, and your chances of closing the deal. Now, take that sheet of paper, fold it in half, and write in big letters – 50%. This represents your potential earnings, as well as your chances of closing the deal, if you have to rely on that second visit. Fold the paper again. As you can see, even the letters aren't as big as when you started. However, the more worrying part is that every time you agree to follow up, your chances of making the sale decreases exponentially. Even worse, you're wasting a lot of time, whereas you could be closing other deals.

As discussed earlier, but worth repeating, a one-call closer must accept the notion that people do indeed make instantaneous decisions. Your job is to help them understand and verbalize that decision, whether it's a "yes" or a "no". Internalize this... A "no" is not only just as good as a "yes," but, at the end of the day, it's worth the same.

**Why are people so afraid of the one-call close scenario?**

It's scary! Or perhaps we have no confidence in ourselves and/or our product or service. A one-call close is an assumptive close. If I'm selling cold bottled water in the middle of the Sahara Desert, I expect only one-call closes. Easy decision, right? Now, you're saying, "but I sell houses, there's no way people will decide on the spot." Why not? Because it's a lot of money, it's not a bottle of water, it's an important decision... You and I probably have contrasting views on which is the more important decision, a new home or water in the middle of the desert, but I'm sure you can see where I'm going with this.

Let's look at it logically. You are showing a home listed for one million dollars. Before you even show the home, have you done your preparatory work? Are you showing the home to all the decision-makers? Are they more or less qualified? If not, then why are you still having the meeting? You are already setting yourself up for failure.

Let's say you have done your homework and you have Mr. and Mrs. Jones in your car, headed for the property. After they've seen the house, while you are still at the property, what do you think the chances are that they have already made a decision? You're probably thinking, pretty low. Or at best they have decided no, or that they need to think about it. Please forgive me, but you are wrong. It's a pretty good chance that before you move on, they've already made the decision. What's a decision? A decision is only one of two things, yes or no! That's it, yes or no, anything else is not a decision. If it's a "no" and you are confident that they really don't want the house, then respect their decision and move on. If it's a "yes," then, have a sales agreement or an offering agreement, or whatever it is you close with, in your industry, ready, and get them to sign. Don't be afraid to ask for a signature today!

You are, now, thinking, this guy is nuts. Nobody says "yes" on a million-dollar home, on the spot, they either say "no" or "we need to think about it." Nobody, and I repeat nobody, needs to think about it. In their gut and heart, they've already made the decision as to whether or not they want the home. In our hearts, we know if this is the home we want to live in, but we have been programed "to think about it."

I hope that, by now, we understand what a "yes" is. But, how do we know what's a qualified "no," and what's just an excuse for not making a decision? First off, a "no" has to make sense! Use your gut. Does it feel right? If they have six kids and it's a two-bedroom house and they say it's too small. What do you think? Do you think that's probably a valid "no"? Then again, if you did your homework correctly, you probably wouldn't have shown them that house in the first place. We will deal with that a little later, but for now, to be a professional one-call closer, you need to have as much information as possible before your sales presentation.

These are all technical things that one can learn. The real challenge that most salespeople have, is they are too scared to ask for a decision. That's the crux of it all! Having the guts and the confidence to simply ask the prospect, whether or not they want this. If they do, then, why not today? Use your logic. Most of the time, if you want something, you want it now. You may say, yes, it's true, I want that brand new Ferrari now, but I don't have the money just yet. Indeed, you might not have the money at that moment in time, but it doesn't change the fact that you want it now. This is why you have to learn to internalize what people are saying.

When people say "no," most of the time, they aren't saying, "no, I don't want it," their underlying voice is "I can't afford it, I can't justify it, I can't see how I can get this or that, etc.… Your job is, first of all, to get them to say, "yes, I want it." A question I like to ask is, "if I was the genie from Aladdin's magic lamp, and time and money were of no concern, would you want this product or service?" If they honestly answer "no," then, that's a qualified "no."

Other than a real "yes" or a real "no," there's only one other option, that's "maybe." Now, I'm sure you get it, we have only three options in sales, "yes," "no," or "maybe." We will continue speaking about "yes's" or "no's" in a bit. But, what's a "maybe?" You guessed it… anything that's not a yes or a no, is a maybe.

Is there such a thing as a valid "maybe"? Yes. A "maybe" is only valid if the prospect still does not have enough information to make a qualified decision, but that is why you are there. But it's a million-dollar purchase, people still have to think about it. You can't expect people to make a million-dollar decision on the spot! Again I ask, why not? Let me ask you a question? If this million-dollar home, for some strange reason, needed to be sold right now and the seller was willing to sell for one hundred thousand dollars, instead of a million. Right now! Yes, no strings attached. Everything is completely on the up and up. Would they take it? Let's also add in the option, that they couldn't sell the house for ten years, so you don't tell me they would buy and resell it. Of course, they would buy it, under the assumption that they were qualified to begin with. The point is simply that when a prospect walks into a home, most people will consciously, or subconsciously, make a decision. I want it. It feels good. They've decided. If the decision isn't "yes," then, it's "no," there is no "maybe." So, what, in fact, is a "maybe?" Other than, that they may still need more information, It's one of two things. Either they don't have the guts to verbalize the decision that they've already made, which means they need your help in making that decision. Or they want it but believe they can't have it. They feel embarrassed to say, "I can't afford it", so instead, they start coming up with excuses, like, "I need to think about it."

A great example for more education, would be this fictitious home we've been talking about. Let's assume that on paper it fits all their needs, wants, and dreams, but it's simply a dump. Run down, needs a ton of work, and the prospect just can't see past the disgusting mess. This is where the real professional salesperson is separated from the clerk.

Our job is to paint the picture. Don't tell them what they can do, paint the picture! Share with them the picture of that snake-infested, overgrown backyard transformed into a mowed lawn of beautiful green grass. The swing set that their children are playing with. The BBQ pit they've built and the fantastic Sunday afternoons they will be spending together as a family. However, in order to do this, you have to believe it. If you do not believe it yourself, then, you're just conning them, you are nothing more than a con-man. In the short run, you may make money, in the long run you will fizzle out and burn. Find out what they want and build it for them! It doesn't matter what you are selling, it's all the same. At the end of the day, you are selling a feeling. If you give your qualified prospect the feeling they want, they will buy.

Not only will they buy, but they will be happy, and you will love your job and make a lot of money. Not just for today, but for the rest of your life.

The problem we face is two-fold. Foremost, we ourselves are afraid to make decisions. For most people, it's just as hard to say "no "as it is to say "yes," if not harder. So, because of that, in almost all of Western society, we almost automatically say, "maybe," or we need to think about it. In certain societies, they are raised from a young age to make key decisions on the spot, but we have been trained "to think about it." How many great opportunities have been lost because "you had to think about it", even when we already knew we wanted to say "yes." Or how many times have we wasted our own time and the time of others because even though we really wanted to say "no," we didn't have the guts? This is where a good salesperson comes in, not to pressure the customer, but to guide them into making a decision. It doesn't matter if the decision is "no," the important thing is for a decision to be made.

# Chapter 7 –
# Selling is a science; it is not magic

Selling is a science; it's not magic. This science is based on logic and communication, so, let's not learn how to sell, let's learn how to communicate. "I know how to communicate," you say. I agree. So, what's the problem, why can't you sell? "It's not the same thing," you say. Well, I beg to differ. Everybody is a born salesman. "Not true," you say. Okay, let's see who's right. For argument's sake, I will assume that if you are reading this book, it means that at one point in your life you were a child. If that assumption is correct, then, we can also make the assumption that you've managed to "sell" an idea of some sort to your parents, teachers, siblings, or friends at some point in your life.

As a professional salesperson, when we want to sell something to somebody, we tend to think it has to be either a product or service. It doesn't matter if you think of yourself as a professional salesperson, or not, you and I are always in the business of selling ideas. It is in our nature as humans to always want to sell an idea to someone. It could be in the process of talking to your spouse, child, parent, friend, boss, and yes, even your customer. Sales is the name of the game and the sooner you realize that regardless of who you are, and what you do, you are a salesperson, the more successful in life you will be. But here's the rub. A lot of people cringe at the idea of being known as a salesperson. Most of us are raised to think salespeople are evil one way or another. Close your eyes right now and give it a thought, when you hear the word, "salesman," what comes to your mind? You probably think pushy, opinionated, someone trying to convince you to buy something you don't need, for twice the price of its worth.

Is that what you do as a salesperson? When you try to sell an idea to your child that it is in her best interest to do her homework, are you doing it for you or her? The truth is you are trying to sell her on the idea because you know it's good for her, and in turn, that makes you happy. In other words, we are not altruistic beings. Life only works properly when it's a win-win situation. Whether it's "real" sales or everyday communication, there has to be something good in it for everybody. So what makes up a good salesperson? It's in fact one who is a great teacher and guide. Our job is to educate the consumer and then, guide them into making the right decision.

My father always taught me, that sometimes to make a point, you have to start off with an extreme. Let's do that. Previously I talked about selling water in the Sahara Desert, so, let's continue with that. A man walking in the Sahara Desert, hot and thirsty; is selling him a bottle of cold, refreshing water immoral? Do we expect it to be a one-call close, or do we expect him to say, "let me think about it", or "I'll get back to you tomorrow?" Of course not, it's an easy decision, he wants the water, he knows it, and you know it. Anything wrong here? Are you being too pushy? Of course not! The only thing that comes into play here is the price. Obviously, the price will be higher than your local town convenience store. Pricing will also make a difference if other vendors are present.

Regardless of what's a fair price, I think we can all agree that the seller believes he or she has a quality product to sell, and the buyer wants that product, now! What if the seller is asking for an exorbitant price, let's say one thousand dollars for one bottle? Now, we have a whole other conundrum, but the fact hasn't changed that the customer has decided he wants the water, the question now is only about price. Without an iota of doubt from either one of us, he will make the purchase for the right price. This is a major point. I want you to take a moment, and let it sink in! Decision and price is a completely separate issue.

Another extreme example... What if instead of water, I was selling cool, refreshing urine. Other than a life and death situation, would anyone buy it? Even for one penny, no! Why not? Because the price is secondary. Foremost, we make decisions based on a yes or no, depending on whether we want something.

Now, I'm sure that you understand the thinking and logic behind one-call selling. It's time to move on and learn the techniques we need to implement. In the next few chapters, we will learn to expect to leave with an answer, and "maybe" is not an answer. Remember, you need to be hungry! As I shared previously, I don't like wasting people's time. If you're given the choice, when would you like to close the sale? If your answer isn't "now, immediately," perhaps, you should consider another career path. The only other sort of acceptable answer is "as soon as possible." Even that, is really not an acceptable answer, but it will do for now. That's usually the answer of people, who either aren't confident in their selling ability, or genuinely believe that their product or service cannot be closed in one call.

Before we go for the gold, remember, nobody likes to be sold anything, but everybody likes to buy. Nobody wants to be pressured or feel like a fool. Almost everybody will tell you they don't make decisions without first thinking about it. This is simply a fallacy, most people make their decision in seconds, they're just afraid to act on it.

If indeed, this is the case, how do we change people's mindsets from being sold, to one of wanting to buy? In every transaction, there is a buyer and a seller. If I were to ask you, which one are you? You would say it depends. On what? Well, whether I am in my professional mode or I am off-duty. The truth is, salespeople are like police officers, which means we are on duty twenty-four-hours-a-day. As the saying goes, sell, sell, sell. Well, how about if we do something totally out of the box? Instead of sell, sell, sell, we start to buy, buy, buy!

# Chapter 8 –
# Let's get down to business!

Let's recap what we've learned so far. We are shooting for a one-call close, and to do that we need to do our homework. We need to make sure we are presenting to a qualified buyer, or buyers. Once we have done this, we can schedule our presentation with the simple intent of walking in, and out, with a sale.

"Intent!" Most prospects have no intention of buying today, but we couldn't care less what the prospect says, because it's not up to them. No matter what they say, we are driving this car, they are just along for the ride. In fact, let me go one step further. The prospects that say, "wow I'm so glad you're here because I've been meaning to buy an XYZ widget" are the biggest challenges. They are generally tire kickers. If they really were so intent on buying a widget, why have they been waiting around for someone to come by? On the other hand, when the prospects says, "you are more than welcome to pitch me, but I'm telling you right now, there's no way I'm going to buy today," that's money in your pocket. I almost always sell these guys. Nine times out of ten, again, assuming they're qualified buyers.

Let's now get back to intent. Who needs the intent? We do! Unless we walk in assuming that we're walking out with the signed deal, there's very little chance we will. You have one chance, make it count! The time you make your initial presentation is the most fertile, ripe time to make that sale. The prospect will never be more open, more excited, more ready to pull the trigger as at that moment. Remember, if you walk out without a sale, for whatever reason, your chances of closing the deal have just been cut in half, at the very least.

Don't forget, a one-call close strategy is not about how many calls you make, or even how many sales you make, it's all about your hourly worth. We discussed it earlier, but let's now take the time and figure this out before we go any further. If your total monthly income is $10,000, using an average 30-day month, we'll have 720 hours per month. Remember, our monetary worth is a variable, but time never is... it's the same for everyone. We all have an average of 720 hours per month at our disposal. In our case, if we have a total gross monthly income of $10,000, then that means our hours are worth close to $14 per hour. It doesn't matter what you are doing, be it sleeping, eating, working, or scuba diving in Tahiti, your hourly value is $14. If your monthly income is $5000, cut this in half, and if its $20,000, then, double it. I trust you can do the math. Regardless of your number, your goal should be to increase this number! I repeat! The goal is to increase the value of your hourly worth, not the hours you work or even the hours you play. You can do whatever you want with your hours, but if your hourly number is low, that means you limit the rest of your options. The more you can increase that number, then, the more options you will have in life. When you waste time on anything you don't want to be doing, it means you are squandering your life away and you will never ever recover that lost time. Do you really want to spend your life chasing down deals where most will never close?

Before we go any further, remember ABC – Always Be Closing! Our mindset needs to be," I am a one-call closer". In everything I do! In every facet of my life!

But what does that really mean in actuality?

It means I make decisions, and I expect others to do the same. Is this too much to ask? If I ask you about almost anything in life, on a personal, or business level, there are three possible answers, or variations thereof. You already know what they are... "Yes," "no," or "maybe." You ask a woman out on a date. Yes, she says, great, I'd love to! We know what that means. No is just as simple, no means no, again as long as it's a valid no. The only other answer is "maybe," which is not an answer, it's an excuse. She may think she's on the fence, but she is being indecisive, or cowardly. She already knows whether or not she wants to go out with you but is afraid to express her wishes. We cannot accept a maybe, whether it's from a prospective date or a prospective customer. Our job is to get them to make a decision, yes or no. Truthfully, we don't care which, because they are both worth money to us. A maybe is a waste of our time which is something we can't afford. It's a waste of our valuable time and emotions!

Now, here's some homework for you. For the next week, consciously, whenever you are asked a decision-making question, whether in your personal or business life, endeavor to give a "yes" or "no" on the spot. The more you get used to being decisive, the more your inclination towards expecting others to be as decisive with you will grow.

In life, there is very little black and white, so always have it at the back of your mind that we are talking in general terms. There will always be circumstances that don't exactly fit into our parameters, but most will.

As we continue, we will focus on three crucial areas that play important roles for anyone who wants to become a one-call closer. They are:

- WIIFM
- Assumptive close
- Open-middle-close

Pay close attention to each chapter and don't skip over anything!

# Chapter 9 – WIIFM

WIIFM are not call letters for a radio station out of New York City, it's an acronym that stands for "what's in it for me?"

Up until this point, I've mentioned several important things to remember, however, this is the most important life lesson I can imprint on you. Everybody, and I mean everybody, has some form of the WIIFM gene inside of them.

Let's not talk about everybody, let's talk about you! Every day, from the moment you awake in the morning till you put your head down on the pillow at night, you are consciously, or subconsciously asking yourself, "what's in it for me?"

I realize that this is a very hard concept to internalize, but it's true. You may need to take some time and let it sink in, but we are all basically selfish beings. We foremost care about ourselves. Don't panic, this is not necessarily bad. In fact, if we didn't care about ourselves first, this place we call earth would be a pretty desolate, and boring place. Every discovery or invention, no matter how altruistic it may seem, only came into existence because someone first asked, "what's in it for me?" I can't help others before I've helped myself, and I can't help myself unless I believe there is something in it for me.

Now, this "something in it for me" doesn't have to be grandiose, it can be as simple as getting out of bed in the morning to go to the bathroom. I may also do something for no other reason, other than it makes me feel good, but I still do it because there's something in it for me. So, am I saying that there are no selfless acts? Yes, that is my opinion.

I give charity or do good deeds because there is something in it for me. Maybe I get a good feeling or perhaps I feel I am improving the world which will ultimately help me or my children. Good point, what about your children? When you do things for your children, are you also being selfish? Theoretically, yes, but let's not focus on the word selfish. Focus more on WIIFM. No matter what I do for my children or those I love, ultimately, there is something in it for me. This is not necessarily, and usually, not a conscious thought or decision, but it is none the less true. Let's take for example what I think might be the most extreme example. That is giving one's life to save another. How can I say that this is not a selfless act? Because no rational person would willingly give up their life for anybody or everybody on this planet. When someone consciously risks their life for someone else, it is not random. It's for an ultimate goal, which seems in the savior's eye to be good for them at the time.

The savior has decided there is a good enough reason to give up their own life. That reason may simply boil down to love, for instance saving the life of their own child. On the flip side, someone who commits suicide, while perhaps not being rational, also thinks, first, WIIFM.

But we are indeed straying, Let's not make this complex or feel like rocket science. Remember, this is supposed to be a simple book about closing a sale in one call, not the meaning of life. Which brings us to the point of WIIFM. If you want to convince anybody of anything, you must first be able to answer, what's in it for them? I wrote this book, why? Obviously, I believe there is something in it for me? You are reading it, why? You obviously believe there is something in it for you. Truly, this is a win-win! When you have a suspect that you are trying to convert to a prospect, that is the number one question that must be answered. If you can master this, then over 50% of your job is done.

# Chapter 10 – Assumptive close

An assumptive close is exactly that, one in which you assume the outcome. Normally, when someone assumes anything, they end up making an ASS/of U/and ME. That would indeed be the case here if our assumption was that we were just expecting a yes. But that's not our assumption. What we assume is that we will get a definitive answer, in other words, a "yes" or a "no". As we discussed, we are just as happy with a "no" as a "yes," just not a maybe.

Whether it's business or personal, when I ask someone a question that involves a commitment, I expect an answer. If it's not a "yes" or a "no," I will naturally want to know, why not? Even if it's a "no," if it makes little sense to me, then, I'll also want to know, why not? To go back to my earlier example, when this guy was trying to sell me a television subscription. Assuming I was the salesperson, if I truly believed that I had a great service, then, I'd have approached the person with the enthusiasm that if he said anything but yes, I would have been truly shocked. That being said, being an experienced salesperson, I would also realize that the average prospect will just say no, or, not interested, as a knee-jerk response. This means, that anything but a "yes," would not satisfy me, because I started out expecting a "yes."

Remember, we will accept a qualified "no," and even cherish it, but I'm still going into this presentation assuming that anything but a "yes" is unacceptable. For the most part, I would be correct. Regardless of the excuse, I'd hold my ground, continuing until I got that coveted "yes," or a qualified "no". Did that guy (yes, I'm intentionally not calling him a "salesperson," so, "guy" should do it), get a qualified "no"? Of course, he did. I don't own a television, nor do I want one. You can't get any more qualified than that. But instead of being a salesperson, he was a robot and continued. What a complete waste of everybody's time? I hope this is getting clearer. "No's" are great, as long as they are qualified. When you receive one, thank the prospect for their time with the same enthusiasm as if it was a "yes," and move on. Of course, not before you have asked for a referral which we will talk about a little later.

I trust we are now clear on what a maybe is. I know we are clear on what a yes is, but what's a no? No is a no! It's a very clear decisive answer, that I don't want whatever it is you are selling. This being said, in order for us to be clear about what a "no" is, we need to clarify with the prospect. We need to make sure that not only is it indeed a "no," but it's an educated "no". Remember, when your prospect has made a real decision, it's virtually impossible to change their mind! This being said, the majority of the time, even the "no" is really a "maybe." It's a knee jerk reaction, the prospect hasn't made a decision. He or she is afraid and automatically says "no."

How do we know if the "no" is real, or a knee-jerk response? First and foremost, you need to listen, afterward, ask questions. If you were the television satellite salesperson, and I told you I don't own, nor want a television, would you agree, that is a real no? I said no and gave you an educated reason. If I had just said no, I'm not interested, that tells us nothing. Time for an obvious follow up question, why not? If the answer is, I don't own, nor want a television, then you have a real "no". But what if he says, I'm happy with my current provider, is that a real no? No! Not as far as we're concerned. All he is saying is that you haven't given him enough of a reason to say "yes." You can't change a person's mind, but you can give them additional information in order for them to make an informed, educated decision, and change their own mind. You have the right to expect an answer to your question, and until the prospect gives you a real answer, you don't leave. Most people will not give you a definitive answer, they are too scared. This is from years of programming. In fact, most people find it easier to say "yes" than "no," and this is to your advantage.

Our job as a one-call closer is to expect either a real "yes," or a real "no", and we will not leave until we get it. This exercise is where we separate the men from the boys. The boys will be afraid to push the envelope, and will settle for a maybe, like "come back tomorrow", or "I need to think about it". The boys are scared that if they stand their ground, they will lose the sale. Maybe they will, but it's more likely that they won't. Stand your ground! I guarantee that in the long run, you will make a lot more money. Go for "yes" or "no" decisions, rather than "maybe's."

Quick review

We have now learned the logic behind a one-call close, and have learned who a suspect is, as well as who a prospect is. In addition, we've scheduled our presentation and we're in. What's our mission now? Very simple, we will not leave this meeting without a bona fide "yes" or "no," nothing less!

Now, let's learn how to do it.

# Chapter 11 – Open-Middle-Close

Many salespeople go in with a canned presentation which is for amateurs. A professional goes in with a planned presentation.

There are two things to ingrain in your brain to become a successful one-call close salesperson. First, you must have a plan, and secondly, you must know how to carry on a conversation.

Your plan, any plan, needs to be simple. The simpler, the better. Having a plan is not enough, it needs to be a plan in which you can work. Your plan must have a beginning, a middle, and an end. Again, all very simple. But without all three and in the proper order, you are setting yourself up for failure.

**Let's review. To become a successful one-call close salesperson, you need to know how to have a conversation, to have a plan, and to be ready to leave the meeting with a "yes" or a "no."**

Open-middle-close; Each one is an integral part of the process. If you skip one or two of the parts, you'll most probably blow the sale. If you run them in a different order, you will also probably blow the sale. Just follow these simple instructions, and you will close more sales than you could have ever imagined.

It is indeed very simple, but sometimes the simplest of things are what mess people up. There is an old acronym, KISS, keep it simple... If you want to succeed, don't complicate things, just follow the plan. When I say follow the plan, I am referring to every part of the plan, not bits and pieces. Don't pick and choose, follow every part. Don't skip over any of the parts and don't rearrange the order. I can't over-emphasize how important it is to just follow the plan – Open-Middle-Close. Most people reading this book will not follow this simple advice and will fail.

They will claim, yes, I read the book, but it didn't help me at all. That's the 80%, but today choose to be part of the 20%, those that will be very successful. The only difference being, one followed the plan while the other "knew better." Where do you want to be? In the 80% or the 20%. Even if you think I'm smoking something, try it for ninety days; what have you got to lose? I challenge you! If you've followed this simple plan for ninety days and you haven't seen any improvement, let me know.

# Chapter 12 – Open

A one-call closer does not engage in small talk or meaningless ice breaker conversations. A one-call closer is there to do a job, not to waste his or her time, nor the prospect's. To be a one-call closer, you must master the art of conversation, which starts with knowing how to listen. Not just with your ears, but with your heart. If you can learn to keep your mouth shut and let the prospect do most of the talking, he or she will tell you all you need to know to help you close the deal. The purpose of the open is to make a friend. Friends like to do business with friends! So the purpose of the open has three goals, and three goals only.

First and foremost; to make a friend…

Having a conversation, seems simple enough. We all know how to have a conversation, we do it all the time. We converse with our partners, friends, children, and co-workers. But for some reason, we become tongue-tied when we are in front of a prospect. There are guys I know who can walk into a bar and start chatting with any woman in there but put him on the phone with a prospect and he sounds like an idiot. What happens to us? Why is it so hard for us to have a simple conversation with a prospect? It's not rocket science, it's simply FEAR. We're scared! Of what? Failure, success, embarrassment, rejection, who knows? And quite frankly, who cares? If you want to be successful, you simply have to learn how to have a conversation with anyone, anywhere. What's a conversation? According to the dictionary, it's a talk, especially an informal one, between two or more people, in which they exchange news and ideas. That's it, again it can't be any simpler. Stop worrying about the sale, you're not here for the sale, you're here to have a conversation.

The first goal of the open is to make a friend, and we do this by having a conversation, not engaging in small talk. The difference between having a conversation and small talk is to be talking about something which is of genuine interest to the prospect, i.e., not the weather or the rising price of goat's milk (unless you're talking to a goat farmer). The second goal of the open, is to leave the open knowing exactly what our new friend wants. Last but not least, the purpose of the open is to get to the middle. What the purpose of the open is not... It is not to make your presentation, nor to close the deal.

This is all about what we refer to as the "open." I keep using the word "simple", but obviously, it's not so simple. If it were, there would be no need for this book. Everybody would be a one-call closer and the 20% wouldn't be raking in all the cash. Let's dissect this and figure out what having a conversation entails.

This is a very simple process, KISS! Do not deviate from this simple recipe! I can say this until I'm blue in the face, but there will always be those who "know better" and will not listen. They will move parts around or skip parts. I advise you once again, should you not follow this formula exactly, you will most probably fail.

In this beginning process known as the "open," before proceeding, you must be certain that the person, or people, in front of you is/are qualified. I know I'm repeating myself, which may seem annoying, but ten extra seconds of reading, is a lot easier than wasting an hour on a meeting that can't lead anywhere.

Have you gotten an affirmative answer to these two simple, but crucial questions? Can the person in front of you legally make the decision? Can they figuratively or literally sign a check?

One of the most common questions I get is, how long should this part take? As long as it takes, this is the most important part of the sales call. You have to decide, whether to continue to the next stage – the middle, or to bail out. Why would you bail out at this point? If at any point you find out that he or she is really not the decision-maker, or you do not have all the decision-makers in front of you, STOP and reschedule. No matter what, do not continue. Making a sale is like driving a vehicle, there can only be one driver at a time. If you are driving, and in the middle of your journey the passenger grabs the wheel, what will happen? Obviously, you will have an accident. It's the same thing here, if you fail to maintain complete control, and allow the prospect to grab the steering wheel, you will have an accident, and crash.

At no point in the "open" stage do you discuss your product or service and never ever discuss price. So, when do you know it's time to move on to the "middle" stage? LISTEN, your prospect will tell you. When you feel comfortable, that he or she has given you a want or a need, you can than start thinking about moving on. In order to move from the open stage to the middle stage, you must have discovered their burning desire, and/or pain point, a.k.a., the power point.

In order to close in one call, you must master the art of listening. Follow the 80/20 rule, which means you are talking 20% of the time, and listening the other 80% of the time. Your goal is to discover your prospect's desires, needs, or wants. In other words, what is their dream or pain point? It doesn't matter whether it is a negative or positive point. If their need, or want, is strong enough that they are ready to do practically anything to get it, then and only then, should you be ready to move on. How long will this process take? It all depends, it can take five minutes or an hour. Depending on the scope of your product or service, an entire presentation should usually take no more than an hour, so ideally, you want each part of the process to take twenty minutes. This is a suggestion but not vital. What is vital is that you don't move on until you know for sure that you have pinpointed their burning desire or pain point!

The other thing that is very important at this stage is to reconfirm their time commitment. Before your meeting starts, you need to get a "time commitment." So, for instance, if your presentation does indeed take an hour, it is incumbent on you to ask the prospect, upon scheduling, to set aside at least one hour for this meeting.

If, you have done everything correctly, but when you get to the meeting, he says that his wife is about to give birth, and he can only give you a few minutes, then you reschedule. You have to realize that you only have one shot at a one call close. Once you've blown your wad, it's blown and can never be recovered. If you have to reschedule, that's fine, it will still be considered a one-call close. If though, you're already halfway through, in the middle stage, and end up rescheduling another meeting, then, it's considered a second call. Remember a second call automatically cuts your chances of success in half.

While we don't really want to reschedule, many times, it works in our favor because now the prospect feels like they owe us something, and they feel a little guilty. Because they had to reschedule, they will treat us more positively. Many times, a rescheduled visit takes the edge off, and it becomes a much easier one-call close. In fact, if you are sensitive to the prospect, he or she will appreciate it. The one caveat at this point is to never lose control. Don't let the prospect rush you or convince you to get on with it. They may say, they already understand, or they may even say, I know I want it, just give me the price. No! Do not be fooled, you will not close the deal. He will say, "thank you, but I got to go because my wife is in labor. Don't worry, I'll get back to you." Chances are, that you'll never speak to him again. He no longer needs you. He thinks he has all the information. This is the crux of the challenge you have.

You are not a salesperson; you are an educator. For you and me, the bulk of the job involves educating the prospect. Just like the slogan from Sym's Clothing, "An educated consumer is our best customer." So true. Because, if the prospect already truly understood what your product or service could do for them, they wouldn't need you. They would just pick up the phone and order it. There would be no need for salespeople, just clerks who take orders. Rather our job is a very serious, professional job; our job is to educate.

**Practical Advice**

Upon the start of the meeting, you want to requalify both the prospect and their time commitment to the meeting. You will then move onto a "very brief" introduction about who you are. Immediately thereafter, you start asking the prospect questions about anything that you think will get them to start talking. That is your mission at this moment, to get the prospect to talk. About almost anything. Not about the weather, nor the traffic. If this is a meeting that you've prepared for, then part of your preparations should be about the individuals involved, not just the company and its business interests. Something that you think may truly interest them, personally! Look around their office, what stands out? Pictures, awards, certificates, memorabilia… it doesn't matter what, just try to avoid talking business. You want to take their mind as far away from their business as possible. Right now your mission is to get them to start talking about themselves. Everybody likes to talk about themselves! Just get them talking! As your prospect starts talking, you start listening. Really listening. If you will focus on what he/she is saying, they will guide you to the right path, in which you will discover their pain point or burning desire, a.k.a., their power point. Remember they should be doing most of the talking throughout the open, at least 80%. The only time, you should be opening your mouth is to enable them, to continue sharing with you. In the "open", you should not be sharing or telling them anything. The only time you should be talking is when you ask them a clarification question. Or you need to prod them along to continue sharing.

To be successful in the open just remember to focus on the prospect and listen intently. Be interested, and try and learn every nitty, gritty detail of his/her power point.

Before we go on, I must reiterate that if for any reason you cannot complete part one of this three-part process, then stop. Either bail out or reschedule. Sometimes, you will run into tire-kickers who will be obnoxious and not let you do your job. WALK! I know it's hard but trust me. If you lose control, there is no way you will close the deal. You'll only waste your time and walk away with negative karma. There will always be jerks, and there is nothing you can do about that. But what you can do is decide whether or not you will allow it to affect you. Cut out early and go sell the next guy.

Let's review. In this first stage called the "open," our job is to one, determine if the prospect is a qualified decision-maker. And two, to discover their power point; in other words, their pain point or burning desire. Again, very simple, but sometimes difficult for us, so let it sink in. Remember, we do not continue under any circumstances to the "middle," if we haven't checked these two boxes off.

# Chapter 13 – Middle

We are now ready for what most people call "the presentation." One-call closers are not ordinary people. Remember, we are in the 20% club, so the average salesperson will not follow this formula. That's okay, because the elite 20%, close 80% of the sales, and earn 80% of the money. As we continue, always keep in mind that we're just having a conversation with the prospect, we are not selling him anything; we are friends. Remember nobody likes to be sold, but everybody likes to buy.

Continuing our conversation with our prospect, we are now proceeding to provide the ideal solution to his/hers, power point. The prospect, really, couldn't care less about us, our company, and believe it or not, our product or service. All he or she cares about is what's in it for them. How are you going to make that searing pain go away, or make that burning desire come true? That's all they care about! So, don't start by going through the canned presentation you were taught. Don't start showing them all the super-duper features of your vacuum cleaner. Why would you even mention the carpet shampooer if they don't have any carpets? Always think, what's their power point? Maybe bed bugs? Maybe all the dirt that forms deep in the crevice of their mattress? What's important is what matters to them, not to you. If that's their pain, then, that's all you should care about, that's what really counts!

Solve their pain, build their dream! That's how you win them over! What you like or think is totally irrelevant. Remember, it's the benefits, not the features that sell. And it's only a benefit if it will benefit them. All this should be really smooth because you are just continuing a conversation that started at the "open" and has now seamlessly transitioned to the "middle." Hence, the importance of following the process in the right order.

Once you have discovered their power point, that's all you should discuss. Every other sentence should have you mentioning their dream or pain point. For example, "do the bed bugs attack you every night or just a couple of times per week? There is only one of two answers, both are great. Regardless of how they answer, you respond along the lines of "I understand, so what you're saying is if we could find a way to get rid of these bed bugs biting you today, you'd want to get started today, right?" All they care about is getting rid of those bed-bug bites ASAP, and now that's all you care about. That's all you talk about. Their current pain, and how you can provide instant relief for that pain today, now! They don't care that the vacuum cleaner is imported from Tanzania or has a twenty-seven-year warranty. All they care about is getting rid of the pain today!

A want is the same thing. If they want it bad enough, can they taste it? Let's say it's the dead of winter in Alaska and you're selling an air conditioning unit? Why should they decide today? They have all winter. Well, you could give them all sorts of logical reasons. Beat the rush, a winter sale, etc., all very good… But all of this lack any emotional tie-in and regardless of what we all believe, we are not logical beings, rather, emotional beings.

So, how do we get them to make the decision today? By making them feel the heat! You must get them, not only, to remember how miserable it was in the heat last July, but the refreshing feeling of coolness as they are sipping their ice-cold lemonade with not a single drop of sweat about. It's all about their feelings! And that's all you should be talking about.

As you continue in this "middle" stage, you are continuously asking assumptive questions. How comfortable will you feel when sleeping in a climate-controlled room? How nice will it be to once again get a comfortable full night's sleep? Just imagine, catching that 11 foot Atlantic blue marlin off the coast of Kona, Hawaii! Be detailed, get into their power point along with them. Get them agreeing to how great that would be. Every question you ask them, you want to hear them say, yes, yes, yes! Paint the picture of that miserable sweltering heat, and then figuratively, cool them down in a way they never ever imagined.

The "open" was all about finding out what their burning desire or searing pain was. Sometimes, as in the case of the air conditioning in Alaska, it may be a bit of both. The middle is all about getting them to admit, that if you can give them their dream or take away their pain, "they would want it today!" How long does the middle take? As long as it takes for you to ask the question, "Mr./Ms. Prospect, if I can bring you relief today? Or if I can get you on the way today to ensure that when you retire, you will be fishing in that 40 ft. cabin cruiser off the coast of Spain, would you be ready to get started right away?" It's all about today, there is no tomorrow! You must be as specific as possible. Don't just say a fishing boat, get into details. Part of your job in the "open" stage was to get as many specifics as possible. Keep building on those specifics and keep reminding them of their dream. Paint that picture and never stop adding colors!

**Practical Advice**

Going from one stage to the next is all very subtle and should be seamless. Just as when you converse with a friend or loved one, you do not consciously think of where one stage stops and one begins, but it happens none the less. We need to take as long as we need in each stage, but once we've accomplished our task we need to move on ASAP. In the open, we know it's time to move on when we feel we have made a friend. When we know that our new friend has opened to us, and is sincerely sharing their searing pain, and/or burning desire.

As we then seamlessly move into the middle, the most notable thing that happens is that we, rather than the prospect, are now doing the majority of the talking. It is now that we make our presentation, but always with "WIIFM" in the forefront of our mind. Again forget all the wonderful features you've been taught, just focus on the benefits which will appeal to the prospect. While the middle is about explaining what we are selling, it is only as far as "What's in It for Them?". Every word out of our mouth needs to have that focus, and every question we ask the prospect has to have a combination of our product/service, along with their power point. These questions have to be rhetorical questions and always include now, or today. We have to confirm the sense of urgency. Once we have the prospect saying yes, to almost every question, or answering our choice questions affirmatively, we know we are there.

During the middle, your job is to constantly reinforce the bridge between what you are selling, and your prospect's power point. For instance, if you are selling vacuum cleaners, and you know your prospect suffers from asthma, you should be constantly putting the two together in practically every sentence. The same would go, if you are in the investment or retirement business, and you know your prospect's dream is being able to cruise around the world. It really doesn't matter what you are selling or what your prospect's power point is, it's all about the equation; product/service + power point = Sale.

Once you feel that they are practically begging for a solution to their power point, then, and only than are you ready to move on to the close.

As I explained earlier, this will all only work if we go by the numbers. Now, what does it take to complete the "middle" stage and move on to the "close" stage?

KISS! A very simple, uncomplicated answer. We must have a firm commitment that if we can give them what they want, can meet their needs today, that they are ready to go ahead, today!

You can ask this segment's closing question in many different ways, but the bottom line is that they are saying, "yes, if you can make my pain go away or my dream come true, I'm in." Without exaggeration, there have been many times that I've gotten to this stage where the prospect had very little idea about what I was even selling. I don't recommend that, but you have to understand that if you've done your job right, they wouldn't care about what you're selling, all they would care about is that it's the answer to their power point. Now, let's assume, that you think you've done everything right and your prospect still says "no!"

"No, I really like you, but regardless, I won't be deciding today." No problem, everything is good, because remember, you're not trying to sell him anything anyway, you're having a conversation with a friend. Not only that, if you have been paying attention, you still have not even asked the prospect to buy anything.

So, if you, indeed, were just having a conversation with a friend, what would be your natural response? "Why? I don't understand, John! "If we can start relieving your pain today, why would you want to wait? It doesn't seem logical." And it's not. So, that means one of two things. One, either you haven't done your job right, or you went too fast, and really didn't find out their power point. Or, you are right on point, but he is still afraid, and not ready to move on to the next stage. This is a very crucial point. If you move to the close stage before your prospect is ready, you will lose the deal. Don't waste time, don't procrastinate, but don't rush it either. Just like you can't skip or rush a stage, you rarely can go back either. Take as long as you need, but don't move to the next stage until you've received a firm commitment.

You need to know that he is so pumped, that if you can indeed fulfill his wishes, he is ready to pull the trigger, now, TODAY! Not getting the answer you want on the first try is normal, it's no big deal. Just go back and rework his or her power point. It doesn't matter how many times you need to, you're in no rush. You're there to solve their problem and you know you've got the answer. Just like a friend who needs your help, you aren't going to abandon him. No matter what he or she says, you're in the driver's seat. You are not going anywhere until you have helped your friend.

Now that you feel that you have completed the "middle" stage, and feel ready to move on, then, ask the closing question of the "middle" stage. There are two closing questions, one for the "middle" stage and one for the "close" stage. The closing question for the "middle" stage is something along the lines of, "Mr. Jones, if we can get you on the way today to ensure that when you retire, you'll be fishing in that 65 ft. Marquis cabin cruiser off the coast of Spain, would you be ready to get started right away?" When he says "yes," this is your cue to transition from the "middle" to the "close" stage.

# Chapter 14 – Close

If you have followed the program without falling off the tracks, this third and final stage should be very easy, easier than you can ever imagine.

Remember, you are not selling anything, rather, you're having a conversation with a friend, trying to help them solve a problem. It may be emotional for them, but for you, everything is logical. It's all so simple because up until now, it has been a very logical sequence of events. You started at the beginning, known as the open, became friends, and discovered their power point. You, then, continued having your conversation through the middle, and dream-built with your friend until they could taste that which they truly desired. They are now practically begging you to make their dream come true, or make their pain go away. You know that you have the answer to their desire, the pill for their ailment, so, it's a no-brainer. This has got to be a win-win situation. They want what you have, you want them to have it, there couldn't possibly be any problem, could there?

Assuming you know how to follow simple instructions, then you've arrived here safely, perfectly poised to cap it all off. It should be smooth sailing from here on. Unfortunately, most people still fail at this point. They'll choke up and drop the ball. Very simply, fear takes over and they lose control of the vehicle. This is where the 80% lose control and go off the road. They are almost at the mountain top, they can see the deal being made, but they simply freeze and let all those insecurities creep in. Their insecurities convince them that nobody decides on the first call, and if they ask for the sale at this point, they'll either lose the sale, and/or make a fool of themselves.

It's time for you to decide, are you going to be in the 20% or the 80%? I don't know if you've realized by now. One of the big differences between a one-call closer, and the rest of the pack, is that a one-call closer is always in control, rather than the prospect. We determine our own destiny; we don't leave it to others.

I know you want to be in the 20%, so trust me! I know what I'm talking about, I've been there. Do it one time, it will be easier the second, then the third, etc., until it will become as natural for you as having a conversation with a friend.

Bite the bullet, take the plunge, and move on. If you've done your job correctly, then, you know that logic is on your side, and the prospect has to say "yes." Go ahead and close the deal. There's no other logical answer. As far as you're concerned, you're closing the deal. There is no other alternative. He or she has been telling you for the past forty-five minutes that they want an answer, a solution, and here you have it.

You are probably confused about now. I can imagine that you're asking yourself, "where exactly are we right now? This is supposed to be the start of the "close" stage, right?" But it is all very subtle, so it's hard to know where one stage begins, and where one ends. This is supposed to be subtle because you are not in the middle of a canned sales presentation, you're just having a conversation with a friend and this naturally progresses from one stage to another. Here are the stages spelt out...

1. To make a friend and find out what their searing pain or burning desire is. In other words, their power point... a.k.a. The Open.
2. To share with your new friend; the benefits of your product and service, and how acquiring it will bring them closer to their power point... a.k.a. The Middle.

3. To bring it all together and have your new friend make the commitment to acquire your product or service for them to achieve what they want! a.k.a. The Close.

## Practical Advice

While the "open" stage is the most important stage of the sales process, if you have done everything correctly, the "close" stage should be the easiest of all the stages. There are two closing questions, one for the "middle" stage and one for the "close" stage. Ideally, we ask, one right after the other. When he says "yes, I want whatever it is today", this is your cue to transition from the "middle" to the "close" stage. We start the close stage, by simply asking the closing question of the "close" stage. When you start the "close" stage, the first sentence out of your mouth should be an assumptive close question. Such as, "would you like to pay cash or pay in installments? Visa or MasterCard? Blue or red? Would you like five widgets or an even dozen?" etc... The idea is that if he goes for any of the options you have pitched, he has, in essence, said "yes!" Another very successful way to close at this point is to take out your order form and ask him or her for their postal code. If they give you the postal code, it's equal to saying, "yes, I'm buying." At this point, about 20% of your prospects will simply say "yes."

Whoa, that was easy! Not so fast. The "close" stage has lots of hidden mines and any of them can go off at any point in time. First, you have to be very sure about what's going on. You have to be very sure of yourself, sure that this is in the best interest of the customer.

For those 20% of your prospects who gave you their acquiesce, you will still only make the sale if you keep control of the situation. That means once they provide an affirmative answer to one of these buying questions, you don't blink. As far as you're concerned, it's a done deal! Don't waste time, don't keep talking, don't ask them if they're sure, don't continue telling them about the product. Just take out your order form or agreement, whatever you use, and fill it out. Once you're done writing it up, ask for their signature, credit card, check, purchase order number, or whatever constitutes a real sale in your business. If they ask a question, answer it, and just continue with whatever you were doing.

Don't pause, blink, or hesitate. You've been given a green light, so don't stop until you have completed the transaction!

Okay, so that's the 20%, what about the rest? The other 80%? Again, if you've done your job correctly, there should be no doubt that you have an answer to their challenge. If at this point, they really start to backtrack and say "no," they aren't sure it will work, or something really negative about your product or service, then, it's either a case of you not doing your job correctly or they're tire-kickers. Either way, your chances of closing are pretty slim, so my suggestion would be to move on. Now, these types of situations should be happening no more than about 10% of the time. If it is more, then, you're doing something wrong, perhaps in your pre-qualification. But stuff happens, and this is part of the business, so, don't sweat it.

Now, this leaves us with the 70%, who are not disqualified and didn't give us a "yes" right off the bat. They told us in one form or another that they are not sure, or that they need time to think about it. An important quality of a professional salesperson is the ability to read people. No matter what people say what they are really saying can be divided into two to four possible answers... 1. Yes, I want it. 2.No, I absolutely don't want it. 3. I think I want it, but I'm not sure, or I'm too scared to make a decision. 4. I'm really not a decision-maker, or the sole decision maker, and I've been messing you around.

Sometimes, during this last part, it may have seemed like they were the decision-maker, but what you didn't know, was that they have a partner or spouse. Even though they still legally may be able to make a decision, they are either under a contractual agreement not to, or they don't have the guts to go it alone. This fourth category will mess you up unless you in fact, have the guts to nail this down preferably when the meeting is scheduled, or at worst during the open. If at any point, you have a concern that they are not the sole decision-maker, then, just ask them. Many times, salespeople are just too afraid to ask. A very simple qualifying question would be; "Mr. Prospect, if I were to show you something today that would double your income, would it be a decision that you could take alone, or is there anybody else you'd need to consult?"

Ask him or her outright. It doesn't matter how outlandish the question is, you're just trying to save both of you time and money. If their answer is that they're not the sole decision-maker, then, that's no problem, just schedule a meeting where all the decision-makers will be present. On the other hand, if you've reached the "close" stage and are just finding out, then, you've blown it. It's probably not going to happen.

So, that takes care of number 4. Number 1, "yes," we've already covered. Now, let's move on and deal with numbers two and three. How do you handle them? Firstly, you must always remember that you are a one-call close professional, and that you're here for a "yes" or a "no". You should accept absolutely nothing else! We've already dealt with "yes", and again if we've done our job correctly, qualified "no's" at this point will be very slim. It is most probably number three, where the prospect is either not entirely convinced or they are too scared to make a decision. If it's a genuine "no," then, you pack up and leave. The challenge though is, how do you differentiate between numbers two and three? In other words, a real "no", or a fake "no"?

There are two things that can happen now, either a question or an objection. For a question, there are two types, a real question or a false flag. How do you differentiate? Let me give you an example. Let's say you entered the "close" stage and pulled out the order form and asked him for his postal code. Instead of answering you, he asks you a question. If it's a very simple straight forward question like, "do you accept American Express?" Or "do you offer next day delivery?" You answer it, and then, go straight back to the order form. If it can't be answered in one or two words, you don't answer it. What do you mean? How can I not answer a question?
This is how we determine if this is a real or false flag question? Let's say you're selling cars and she asks what options are available? You answer, "no problem, I'll get to that in a minute" and you calmly continue filling out the order form. This is the way you generally handle any question throughout your sales call. Unless it's simple and pertinent, you politely ignore it. If they ask the same question a second time, then, you either immediately answer or say you will get to it. Regardless, you must answer it because if they ask a second time, it means it's a real question. You will find that most questions are false flags. The prospect will never bring them up again, because they were really not important to them in the first place. Either way, you must constantly be the driver in control. After answering a question, immediately, get back on course to your ultimate destination.

Before proceeding, let's try to get rid of the genuine "no's." As discussed earlier, a genuine "no" is a real "no". The prospect has absolutely no desire or interest. He has no pain that your product or service can solve and/or no dream it will bring. You should already know this back in the middle and shouldn't have even gotten to the close. If you sell this type of person, you are more of a hustler or con-man and risk chargebacks, returns, and bad press. Follow the plan, and this type of genuine "no" will have been weeded out way before you got through the middle stage. If you're not absolutely sure that you know the prospect's power point, you shouldn't be at the "middle", and for sure, not the "close" stage. If you are, then, you're just another run-of-the-mill salesperson, and your chances of closing the sale today are slim to none.

On occasion, these genuine "no's" will slip through the cracks and my suggestion is to move on. As always, and regardless of how you leave, always try to get at least two referrals of someone that this person thinks might have a need or desire for your product or service.

Try to get as much detail as possible about these referrals. Ask your prospect if you can use their name, and if you have indeed established a friendship, ask the prospect if they wouldn't mind picking up the phone and giving you an introduction.

Let's now move on to our last category, number three. He hasn't given you a firm "yes" or "no," but a "maybe." In the sales world, "maybe's" are known as objections.

# Chapter 15 – Objections

My mentor, the late Zig Ziglar used to say that every sale has five basic obstacles: no need, no money, no hurry, no desire, no trust. If there's no need – you shouldn't be here at this stage and you blew it.

No money – that may be where we indeed are, and we will discuss that.

No hurry – you shouldn't be here at this stage. Did you plant the seeds of urgency?

No desire – you shouldn't be here at this stage and you blew it.
No trust – you shouldn't be here at this stage and it is completely in your hands, but, in fact, this might be where we are.

At this stage of the game, there's a 90% chance that it's all about the money. Another 8% chance that it's about trust, and only 2% that it's about something else. In order to have any chance of closing the deal, we have to know where we stand.

How do we do that? We start by asking, "Mr. or Ms. Prospect, over the past hour, you've shared with me how awful and exhausting your bedbug problem is. You've shared how you would do almost anything to get a good night's sleep. You've shared how if the genie from Aladdin's magic lamp gave you a wish, this would be your first wish, so really, what's the problem?" If as we've discussed throughout this book, you've done your job right, you and your prospect would have become friends. So, talk straight with them. Don't be afraid to ask a direct question.

If they say anything which impugns you, or your company, believe them, because that's their real objection. If it's you, then, you have a serious problem, because it means you haven't been sincere, and they are onto you. You can try to save it, but it's now an uphill battle. If it's about your company, then, it all depends on why? If they simply don't have enough information about your company, give it to them, while assuring them that they are dealing with you, not the company, and that, you've got their back. If you've truly made a friend, you will be able to overcome this objection pretty easily. If it's more serious, for instance, bad reviews, etc., then it will be much harder. Perhaps, you don't want to be working with a company that has such bad press.

Regardless of what their objection is, always ask a confirmation question. "John/Mary, other than XYZ, is there any other reason why you wouldn't be prepared to move ahead, today?" You don't want to be wasting your time on an objection if that's not their primary or real concern. We need to isolate their real objection.

When you ask the genie question, and end with, "so, what's really the objection?" If they say it's a trust issue, well, that, we've just covered. If they say anything else besides a trust or money issue, then, before you answer, you ask the confirmation question. "John/Mary, other than XYZ, is there any other reason you wouldn't be prepared to move ahead today?" If they answer, "nope, that's it," well, either you can, or you can't. For instance, they say, "I want it, but only if you can deliver it by tomorrow." Pretty much, that's it. Can you deliver by tomorrow? If you absolutely can't, then you're probably in trouble.

The only other chance you have is to dig a little deeper to see if it's truly a valid objection. But let's assume you know you can deliver, or you're really not sure, don't answer immediately. This is now your opportunity to seal the deal. Even if you know you can deliver by tomorrow, say to your prospect, "no, I don't think it's possible, but let me ask you a question. If there was any way possible to get the widget to you by 6 pm tomorrow evening, would you go ahead with the deal today?" Always emphasize "today!" If he answers affirmatively, then, you have a deal. If he still says "no," then, you know this wasn't a real objection. If he says yes, and you know you can do it, you still continue with the game. You pick up the phone, call somebody and say, "Hi boss, I'm sitting with Mary Smith and she loves our ABC widget. She really wants it, but there's a serious challenge, she needs it by the close of business tomorrow. I explained to Mary that there is absolutely no way we could deliver by then, but I said I'd call and ask anyway. Please boss, is there anything you can do?" Pause, wait and then say "Boss, thank you so much, you're unbelievable, etc.!" Make sure Mary is within earshot throughout the entire conversation. Get off the phone and with as much excitement as you can muster, look Mary straight in the face, smile and say, "Mary, "we" did it." Without another word, take out your order form, agreement, or whatever, fill it out and give to Mary to sign. From this point on you shut up until Mary either signs or says something. The first one who speaks at this point has bought.

This is a very important point... Throughout this whole process, listening is key. As I've stated already, each step is vital and cannot be skipped. On the other hand, timing is completely up to you. You must listen closely to what the prospect is saying at all times. They will tell you when to move on to the next step and when it's time to close. There are no strict rules here except one, when the prospect is ready, you close. No matter what you were planning to say, drop everything, take out the agreement and close!

If trust issues represent 8% of the objections, and 90% of the objections are about money; does this mean that the other 2% are just technical questions? Let's find out.

As with everything else we've been discussing, a money objection is very simple, and is our most common objection. Our premise is that if they have a real money objection, this means that they want what we're selling. No sane person would want to pay anything for something they didn't want or see value in. Knowing this makes our job all that much easier.

Once you have entered the "close," most of the time, questions and objections are synonymous. They're how the prospect lets you know he needs something else before pulling the trigger. Objections are nothing to fear. If you've done everything correctly up in till now, they are just part of the dance. Just keep remembering this is all about continuing the conversation you're having with a friend. You are just trying to convince your friend to do something which you both know is in their best interest. This is just part of the process. Like questions, there are two types of objections – knee-jerk and money.

Let's start with "knee jerk." Remember, human beings have a very hard time being decisive. It's always very difficult for us to say "yes" or "no". We are programed to always have to "think" about it. The truth is that we usually know, almost immediately, which way we want to go, but find ourselves afraid to verbalize that decision. So, we hum and haw, and most of the time, we make a mistake in starting the thinking process. If you've done your job well up until this point, no matter what they say, you've got an excellent chance of closing them today. You already know that your prospect wants your product or service. It's not even a question, you've asked him over and over, and he has kept saying "yes." They, then, affirmed to you several times that if you can solve their problem or fulfil their burning desire, he or she wouldn't want to wait another day to get started. You've made the sale! Just take a deep breath and make it happen.

How can I be so bold as to make this statement? Because again, if you have done your job, the only reason why you're at this point is that he or she wants whatever you're selling. If there was any doubt, that he or she was not interested, then, you should not be, and would not be at this third stage of "close." If you've rushed or skipped things, then, you may, in fact, be in trouble. If this is the case, you will either now lose the sale or have a rough time re-navigating the waters by backpedaling. I'm sure that's not the case, so, let's continue.

So, what's really the problem? You know he or she wants the cookie. They are either too afraid to make a decision or they see the cost as an obstacle. Remember, no matter what they say, the vast majority of the time, the only real objection is money.

Your job at this point is to help them figure out which it is, and to push them into making a decision. They've told you, so, you're convinced that they really want it; your job is to help them get it. At this point, you have to make it clear to them that they really want it, and it's just about the money. Remember, no matter what they say, it's almost always only about the money.

I can already see the wheels turning in your head, and you're saying, "what if it's something else?" After all, there are other things besides money. Yes, I agree with you, there are other valid objections other than money. But if you have done your job correctly and you are legitimately in the "close," then, I can very comfortably say to you that in the vast majority of the cases, no matter what they say, it's just about the money, or alternatively a trust issue.

Take a moment and think of the last five objections a prospect gave you. They were either true or false objections. A true objection is exactly that, true, and it makes complete sense. For instance, if they say it's too expensive, is this a true objection? To them, it is, to another it might not be. Regardless, this is what we call a "true" objection. Let's say they reply with, "I don't own nor want a car" and you are selling car insurance. Or mortgage insurance and they are renting, etc. All these objections are true, and it's your job to help the prospect say "no," because unless you are a crook, a person who doesn't own nor drive a car, doesn't need car insurance.

On the other hand, you can overcome the price objection because it's subjective. Now again, if they now bring up a really true objection, then, it means you really weren't listening, or they were pulling your leg. True objections are usually objective and should not be coming up now. 90% plus of the time, no matter what they say, no matter how plausible it sounds, at this point in your presentation, it's only about the money.

Ask yourself a very simple question. If from whatever you are selling, you deducted 90% from the price, would they say yes? If you are selling a $1000 item for $100, or a $50,000 car for $5000, would they buy? If you're selling programing services and they don't own nor want a television, then you won't sell them even if you give it away. That's the way you know if it's a real objection, or if it's about the money. In fact, sometimes, that's a great way of closing them. But what happens when they tell you they don't need your programing, because they don't own a television, but you're not sure that's true. Then, you ask, one simple question," Mr. Prospect, if I could give you a year of totally free programing, would you be interested?" If he says no, then say goodbye. If he says anything else, then, you know he's been pulling your leg. You now know it's either one of two things; it's either the cost or he's been lying to you and is not real the decision-maker.

Once you've established that the real objection is cost-related, you can continue. Regardless of what they say, your mission is to continue to solidify in the prospect's mind that he wants the product or service immediately, today! We understand that he is afraid to make that decision, and that's why we're here, to help them. You must, constantly, reinforce the reason they want your help, that you have the answer to their "why." Whether it's the pain point or the dream, no matter what he says, you must keep going back to the power point.

Since we now realize it's just about the money, it puts us in an excellent situation. We are about to close the deal, so let's deal with the money objection.

# Chapter 16 – Money Objections

When dealing with any objection, you must know what you are up against. The money objection is the easiest of all objections because it's simple, as well as being the most common. Our premise is that to have a "real money objection" means that foremost they want what you are selling. No sane person would want to pay anything for something they didn't want or see value in. Knowing this makes your job all that much easier.

When a prospect tells us that our product or service costs too much money, what's he or she really saying? One of three things... I genuinely feel it's too much money for the product or service you provide.

It's too much money for me, or I can't afford it.

I want a better deal.

**Feel, felt, found!**

No matter what the objection is, you start out with these words. For instance, he tells you that yes, he loves the water sprinkling system, but it will have to wait because his wife is about to give birth, and he first needs to talk with her. Well, first, if she, indeed, is a primary decision-maker, then you should have found that out more than an hour ago and rescheduled until she was there. But let's assume he "promised" you that he makes all the home decisions by himself. You first preface your reply with the following phrase. "Mr. Prospect, I know exactly how you feel. When I had a decision like this to make, I felt the same way, but this is what I found." No matter what the objection is, this is the way you start your response. If you feel comfortable using a different version, that's fine, but stick to the formula.

You always want to start out by agreeing with him/her (no matter how stupid the objection might be). You, then, always want to empathize with them, make them appreciate that you know how they are feeling, that you've walked in their moccasins, or something similar. Lastly, you, now, want to give them an answer based on your knowledge and/or experience. You have been partnering with your prospect. It's no longer a question if they will acquire whatever we are selling, just how? "We will figure this out together, because now we are partners in this decision." The prospect has already made the decision, he or she wants to buy, but they need your help because they're scared. In order for us to do that, we must clarify exactly what their objection is.

**It's too much money**

First, always repeat the objection. "Joe/Mary, just so I can understand what you are saying, and please correct me if I'm wrong. You love the product/service, and you are ready to go ahead with it today, but you just feel it's too much money. Is that correct?" Now, shut up and wait! Do not say another word until they answer. It is always very important, but in the "close," it's more important than ever. Always remember, when you ask a question, you say nothing until they answer. Also, don't be too quick to respond. Even after the prospect answers, take a good pause until you respond.

Another important point at this closing juncture, is to constantly work on narrowing down their objection to its lowest common denominator. For instance, if the prospect has told you that it's too much money, so you might want to ask him/her, "are you saying it's too much money to get rid of the bedbugs, that are eating you up night after night, or are you saying, Mr. Prospect, that it's too much money, for you to spend at this time?"

## Reaffirmed, isolated, reinforced

What you did in this closing question was three-fold. First, you reaffirmed that they loved or needed the product or service. Second, you isolated the objection, and lastly, you reinforced, that the deal will be closed today.

If their reply is a "no," go back and ask "why?" A great phrase to use is, "I don't understand!" Because you truly don't. However, if they say "yes," you should say, "I'm not sure I understand, Mary. Are you saying that the cost is too high for this item, or it just doesn't fit in your budget today?"

We are trying to isolate the real objection, but the answer is really irrelevant, because we respond the same way. "Joe, I know how you feel, I remember when I wanted to buy a beautiful painting, I felt the same way. It just seemed like too much money for some paint on canvas, but then, I found that I wasn't just buying a piece of cloth, but I was buying a piece of artwork. This was something that would be mine, plus I would have the undeniable pleasure of appreciating this for many years to come, and then, there is the value appreciation that comes with it."

Regardless of what examples I give, at the end of the day, it is you who has to use your brain and imagination. Once you have reaffirmed, isolated, and reinforced the objection, you, then, go back to an assumptive close.

Continuing with the order, you ask a reinforcement question like, postal code, which credit card, etc., and close the deal. If they still object, you go right back to the beginning, with the "I don't understand", and "feel, felt, and found."

If you've been paying attention, you took note that the money objection we just dealt with was irrelevant to us. We didn't care if he felt the money was too much for the product, or for him. We handled the objection the same way. We concentrated on reinforcing the value. Many salespeople will automatically jump to a peddler mentality and try to give them a better price. Even if you can give them a better price, by you automatically jumping straight to a discount, you will have lost all credibility. That should be your magic bullet and used only as a last resort. Remember, if we've done our job right, then what we are selling them is almost priceless to them, because we are solving their power point. That is why you should keep repeating the "feel, felt, found" as many as five times, each time reaffirming, isolating, and reinforcing the value of the product.

Every response has to focus on their power point. Don't be in a rush to talk about money! Remember, regardless of whatever they say, it's always about the money, but the money is the least important thing to them. What they really care about is their power point. If you have a life-threatening illness, the last thing you are concerned with is the money. Your life is priceless, and you will do whatever it takes to get the money. Unless you are truly selling them something to physically save their life today, this is just an example of why money is irrelevant. Almost anything you are selling can be almost as compelling as saving their life today, if you have truly discovered their "burning desire or extreme pain point."

When you have reached the point where you have reaffirmed, isolated, and reinforced, and you are completely satisfied that they are ready for the final push, then, and only then, do you use your magic bullet.

# Chapter 17 – Magic Bullet

What is the magic bullet?

The magic bullet analogy comes from the old west, when cowboys used to carry a six-shooter, a revolver which carried six bullets. The cowboy always had to remain fully aware of how many bullets were left in his gun, because if he shot off all six, he was dead. After firing five bullets, he knew that he had no other choice, and had to make the sixth bullet count. Failure to do so, and he'd be out of ammunition. The sixth bullet became known as the magic bullet.

Based on this folklore, after you have gone around and round with your prospect, you can consider using the magic bullet. Like the old west, you have to respond to the real objection at least five times before using the magic bullet. Unlike the old west, you can go beyond five times. The thing to remember is that regardless of how many bullets you use, by the time you opt to go for the magic bullet, that will be it! No turning back! You will have no more ammunition left and if you miss, then, you are euphemistically dead. In other words, you will have lost the sale.

There are different magic bullets, and the one you choose to use, will depend on several things. First, what's in your arsenal? What do you have to offer? It boils down to a question of money, terms or extras. The second question is, what is their true money objection? It's usually one of three possibilities. They feel they can't afford it, or believe they don't have the money, (which may or may not be true), they want a better deal, or they feel your product/service is overpriced. It's very important that you don't use your magic bullet, until you are absolutely sure you have isolated their objection down to one thing. Do you know the specifics of their objection?

If it's that they feel they can't afford it, or they believe they don't have the money, then, you have a couple of options; better price or better terms. Never give up everything at first. Always play hard to get by reaffirming, isolating, and reinforcing. Before you offer anything, always say that you don't think it's possible, but you will check into it. This is a psychological game, but it's also completely logical. You must always remain logical. For the prospect, it's emotional right now, regardless of what they say. If they really want what you are selling because they believe it will solve their power point, and they believe they can't have it, they will be feeling very uneasy. They want it, and you want them to have it. The difference, right now, is that they are emotionally involved, and you are not.

Before you offer anything, think from the prospect's point of view. If you could have done this before, and you're supposed to be his friend, why didn't you offer him this deal from the start? That is a legitimate question and I will give you the legitimate answer. This answer is between you and me, not for you to share with your prospect. No matter what, this is really not about the money, it's about the allusion of money. Had you from the start, quoted him, or her, half the price that we are talking about now, we'd still be in this exact same situation; this is human nature.

If it's that they feel they can't afford it, or they believe they don't have the money, then, always, start with better terms.

Regardless, of whether you are offering a discount or better terms, first, qualify every possible monetary objection with the following preface. "Mr. prospect, as I mentioned earlier, this is the price, and even though I wish I could, there are no discounts. However, if there was a way, I could get the price reduced, by as much as X%, would we be good to go, today?"

Another great way of feeling the prospect out, is what I call the "take away" close. Let's say you are selling life insurance, and you have shown the prospect how a one million dollar policy is the answer to his power point. He believes that he can't afford it. So we now say to him, "John, let's go today with just a $700,000 policy, and later on when you can afford it, we will add the rest." This opens up two possibilities. 1) we still close the sale today, with a definite possibility of getting more business later. Or 2) if you have the flexibility, instead of going down in price, you use this as leverage to close the deal today.

Never offer him, or her anything outright, you're just asking hypothetical questions. You don't want to be wasting your ammunition. Learn from politicians, don't offer anything unless you know the answer. Instead send up trial balloons. If the answer isn't yes, that's fine, just go back and start closing them again. You are like a doctor doing exploratory surgery; you are probing. Either they are not serious, or there's another objection that you haven't uncovered. Remember, you have as many regular bullets as you want, but only one magical bullet.

If they say "yes," then, you pick up your phone, call "someone," and get it approved. When you get off the phone, you are as excited as you've ever been. You shake your customer's hand, congratulating them on their new acquisition. It doesn't make a difference what the deal is. It doesn't make a difference if it's money or terms, you go right to the order form and pick up the check.

This works the same way for the guy who "needs" or wants a better deal. The only difference is that with the guy who wants a better deal, try never to give money, but rather, more of something. If you're selling a car, give him some extras. Something that involves time; throw in an extra month at no charge. A free dozen of something, anything but money. He wants a deal, but it's not about money and even if your profit is the same, it's your credibility on the line.

# Chapter 18 – It's all about today!

It's all about today, there is no tomorrow. Your job is to stay with your customer, until they have the courage to finalize their decision.

Your job is to stay as long as it takes for them to say "yes," and to execute the deal.

It's only a question of time. No matter how long it takes, you are not leaving without having that deal signed. It's sometimes a question of wills, but you are not going anywhere. If they really want you to leave, they'll let you know, but this rarely happens. Most people will not kick you out. Most people don't have the guts. They'll either give you a "yes," a "real no," or a "maybe." When they give you a maybe, it means they're too weak to say "yes" or "no," so, they're just hoping you will give up and leave. Don't! You have every right to expect a "yes" or "no". Remember, both are great, and both will make you money.

Regardless of what happens, you are walking out with a definitive answer. If you truly believe this is good for your prospect, then, the answer has to be a "yes." Do you really believe your product or service will improve their life? It doesn't matter whether, or not, it's a necessity. Doesn't matter if it's a luxury. Will it improve their quality of life? If yes, then, you have almost a moral obligation to make sure they buy. You can't leave until they do! You have a responsibility to make sure they have it, today! This may seem a bit overdramatic, but this is what it boils down to. Imagine your prospect is a friend or relative, would you sell it to them? If not, perhaps, you should consider another product or service. If you believe in your product or service, then, sell it today, because your prospect will never be more ready than they are right now.

## My thoughts

I'm a salesman and have always been a salesman. I've had many different titles, from door-to-door salesman, to Managing Director and CEO; but always a salesman. I am still a salesman, but now I specialize in helping others sell their wares and services. I've worked with high tech and low tech, small companies and very large ones. All sorts of different products and services. I love selling and I love helping others do the same! If I can help you, please shoot me an email. freddy@rabbifreddy.com

www.ingramcontent.com/pod-product-compliance
Lightning Source LLC
Chambersburg PA
CBHW070811220526
45466CB00002B/634